15 MOST POPULAR CLASSICAL MELODIES

F HORN

C014102918

Arranged by Michael Whalen

Cherry Lane Music Company
Director of Publications/Project Editor: Mark Phillips

ISBN 1-57560-769-7

Visit our website at www.cherrylane.com

CONTENTS

THE HAPPY FARMER

HORN

By Robert Schumann

IN THE HALL OF THE MOUNTAIN KING
from PEER GYNT

HORN

By Edvard Grieg

JESU, JOY OF MAN'S DESIRING

HORN

By Johann Sebastian Bach

MINUET IN G

from the ANNA MAGDALENA NOTEBOOK (originally for keyboard)

HORN

By Johann Sebastian Bach

MORNING
from PEER GYNT

HORN

By Edvard Grieg

ODE TO JOY

HORN

By Ludwig van Beethoven

PACHELBEL CANON

HORN

By Johann Pachelbel

15

PAVANE

HORN

By Gabriel Fauré

RONDEAU

HORN

By Jean-Joseph Mouret

THE SKATERS WALTZ

HORN

By Emil Waldteufel

SPRING
from THE FOUR SEASONS

HORN

By Antonio Vivaldi

THE SURPRISE SYMPHONY

HORN

By Franz Joseph Haydn

WALTZ OF THE FLOWERS
from THE NUTCRACKER

HORN

By Pyotr Il'yich Tchaikovsky